DEDICATED TO

THOSE WHO BELIEVE IN THE
FREEDOM OF SPEECH
the right to express
opinions without
government restraint

AMENDMENT I
CONSTITUTION OF U.S.A.

 Preface

As I put the finishing touches on this book filled with letters :ten by one person during the Trump-Era, I am even more in awe he letters you are about to read.   In an era where 'untruth's' have ie into being, this book is a compilation of truths that historians rely on for accuracy. Raised in Tulsa, when I heard about the Tulsa e Massacre almost fifty years after graduating from high school, I such disdain for all of the hundreds of people who had done rything they could to keep this horrible event from ever making it he history books.   The history I was taught and believed was irate was no better than the lie hiding the truth.   Truth has to vail. History has to be correct. Publishing Deb's letters do just t. They are the truth of our history and now in print are another e to outlive the untruths.

's Pulitzer-like writing skills have my husband and I rushing each ning to first read the editorial page to see if she has another one ted. Her frequency in print is evidence of the respect she has ied from the editors of our local newspaper. They print her letters iout constraints to the frequency nor the number of words she mits to the newspaper. The impetus to want to publish her letters ie about with one exceptional letter that she wrote.

nds first, her husband, Rick and my husband, Jon have regularly >yed breakfasts for some time. When we get together, we need no

warm-up...we just start in where we left off from our last visit.
although we have topics galore to talk about, our conversat
always include the unsettling politics of our time.

All four of us write letters to the editor and are usually published
not nearly as frequently as Deb...mostly in response to someo
blithering about a lie they are convinced is pure truth. Unbeliev
to even us a couple of times we were published with Deb's.
always, total credit goes to Deb for saying best what we wish
either had the nerve to say or better yet, knows best how to say v
we're thinking.

Deb was excited about the prospect of publishing her letters wh
first brought it up. When she brought her bundle of printed let
on the tiny pieces of newsprint, I was amazed and somew
overwhelmed. I had no idea that she had been published so m
times. That she trusted me enough to give them to me, I felt I sho
have worn white gloves.

She kept publishing while I worked on the book - I think there
about 80 letters with well over 13,000 words. This is her 'story' of
history. And once I committed to write the book and saw how po
the pictures of them looked, I ended up typing every one of her lett
every word. Some letters required more attention than others I h
to admit, but I wanted the corrections for Deb. Not only is Det
excellent writer, she is an eagle eye when it comes to editing. Deb
spent hours and hours going over all of her work that I have typ
Deb is as excited as I am to get her letters published.

Knowing that Deb and Rick were on the Kent campus when
National guard killed four students, Rick coming to the area alm
immediately after the shooting, I can't help feeling might be a rea
that they continue to this day to be so vocal about the truth. T
have seen firsthand, lived firsthand what happens when the poli
go awry. When Deb started her letter writing once they moved h

ubt she gave any thought to how many she would end up writing.
d how could she possibly realize when she started that she was
ting the 'story' of our times in her letters.

ere are other reasons, too, than Deb's excellent writing to have her
ok published.   I am the proud granddaughter of a WWI Vet who
s an American citizen, an immigrant from Italy, who barely spoke
glish. I am the proud daughter of a WWII Vet who served in the
ific on a LST and the proud wife of a two-tour Vietnam Vet.

ey fortunately all survived their tours, all proud to have served their
ntry in the military. But so many of each of their generations died
 the sake of our Freedoms. Deb writing her very truths is because
he Freedom of Speech.   It has been such an honor and privilege
put this compilation of Deb's letters together for others to now
oy reading.

t it is Freedom I believe is under fire. Who would have ever thought
re would be books banned in 2023. Also a proud American, I still
nd proud when the red, white and blue lead a parade or the
tional Anthem is sung at the start of a sporting event. But now in
 senior years, I wonder if I will outlive our democracy.

I do my morning walk, I wave when the lady in the blue SUV
ivers her few papers. Seems like only yesterday it was a young
yclist delivering the newspapers, morning and night to just about
ry driveway. It was how we got our news, how we stayed informed,
d how we stayed in touch with truth, honesty and integrity. We
v the news nightly on only 3 stations... Cronkite, was the epitome
honesty and humbleness. How do people get their news today? By
ebook? Fox? Or more frightening, maybe no news is being heard
sought out.

et a young black man who had just moved here from Florida and
de an assumption in my comment to him that I bet he was glad to
living here now. And I went on to ask him how did it make him feel

to have a Governor suggest that slavery was a good way to help b
character? He had no clue as to what I was talking about. He di
know that black studies had been taken out of the classroom. I t
was shocked, even more so when none of this information seeme
mean anything to him. It was a pointless conversation for both of

Trump, just one man, didn't get our country into this mess. But he
taken full advantage of so many of our weaknesses to line his pock
at the expense of those he has believing he is on their side.

Now, on the opposite end of the spectrum is Deb writing one let
after another, all published, pointing out the faults of the man,
consequences of his hatefulness and giving her words strength to
people to wake up, pay attention and realize we are within inches
sliding down a slippery slope with no return.

To me, now more than any other time in my lifetime, Deb's letters
so important to our country...they are our way of life, they talk of
importance of all of our freedoms and especially of truths. We ca
let happen to our country what history shows is so real, so possi
Deb is doing her part with her letters. Never at a loss for words,
will thoroughly enjoy reading each and every one of her letters fil
with truth, humor at times topped off with a touch of sarcasm a
always...the closing words equivalent to an 'Amen'.

I predict that you will feel the same about Deb's words as I do by
time you finish her book. The most honorable thing you can do w
Deb's words is to pass this book onto someone else, telling them
do the same when they finish reading it.

TABLE OF CONTENTS

x

DEB'S BEST, YET!

MORAL COMPASS DRIVES COMMON SENSE

A recent letter writer says he's struck by liberal letter writers expressing hatred for Trump and disdain for "all things Republican". Let's see – Donald Trump - so much to love! Incited deadly insurrection. Called for violence against his VP. Putin supporter. Serial liar. Still spouting The Big Lie. Sowing massive distrust in elections. Adulterer and woman assaulter. Downplayed COVID, resulting in many unnecessary deaths. Science denier. Bully who attacks anyone who disagrees with him. Now promising to dismantle our government and set up fascist regime if elected. Feel the love? On to disdain for all things Republican. To name just a few: science denial, voter suppression, spreading the Big Lie, culture wars, gerrymandered districts, book banning, war on women, war on LGBTQs, war on public education, blatant racism, normalization and acceptance of the attempted coup by a sore loser president and his supporters. Disdain? Far too weak a word for anyone possessing a working moral compass.

Published July 26, 2023

UNPRESIDENTIAL
TRUMP BEING
UNPRESIDENTIAL

TRUMP PRACTICES TRANSFERENCE

"Wacky". "Pompous Fool." "Not something we are thrilled with." "A very stupid guy." These retaliatory words were recently used by President Trump to express his opinion of Britain's ambassador to the U.S. This childish response to some unflattering but oh-so-true leaked remarks by the ambassador, about POTUS and his administration. How very ironic that our president used terms and descriptions that so aptly describe himself! I believe in the world of psychology this is known as transference...the attributing of one's own traits to another.

Published August 19, 2019

THANKFUL TRUMP WASN'T PRESIDENT DURING WWII

Re: the Jan. 9 letter "Thankful these Dems weren't around in 1941."

Who would ever believe that President Trump and his adoring circle of lock-step Republicans would have been competent leaders during World War II?

FDR would be rolling in his grave at the thought. We should all be very thankful that someone with Trump's arrogance, ignorance, ineptitude, lack of qualifications and total non-interest in advice and input from his own experts was not sitting in the Oval Office at that crucial moment in history.

CARTOON PROMPTS
THE WRONG QUESTION

Re: the March 30th letter to the editor, "Cartoon was disgusting."

The author of the letter was upset over the drawing showing President Dennison – oops, I mean President Trump - getting spanked by special counsel Robert Mueller. She is worried about children not understanding someone being "spanked by a magazine." What are they to be told? Seriously?

Might the more appropriate question be, what might our children think when they read about the president of the United States hooking up with a porn performer (while married), and his other lewd and crass behavior toward women?

Or does the letter writer, following suit with Trump, think the media and the truth should be squelched and buried?

TOXIC LEADERSHIP, TOXIC DERAILMENT

Re: the Feb 25 article "Railroads fought to crush some safety rules."

The horrific toxic rail disaster not far from my hometown in Ohio has occupied the national news. What long-term cost to human, animal and environmental health? During his first year in office, Donald Trump bragged about getting rid of more "unnecessary safety regulations in just 12 months than any other administration during their full term." This included rail transport regulations of hazardous materials. According to Trump, regulations "slow the economy." Experts on rail safety warned of "an unprecedented new level of risk for American cities."

East Palestine, Ohio is now experiencing the consequences. The rural community of about 5,000 with an average income of $40,000, voted overwhelmingly for Trump— 71%. Perhaps some thought will be given to a candidate's values and priorities after this toxic disaster, but I doubt it. It's a chilling example of what ignorantly voting against one's own best interests can manifest.

ELECTION REVIEW HAS CARNIVAL FEEL

Re: the May 16 article "AZ's kooky election audit."

Several letters ask why Democrats don't welcome the 'audit' going on in Maricopa County. They assume this 'audit' is legitimate and professional. Please read Tim Steller's article "AZ's kooky election audit" to get a clue of what is really going on.

Any honest person knows Joe Biden was elected fairly and legitimately, as affirmed by courts across the country. Why would anyone want to lend credence to Trump's Big Lie by supporting this "fraudit" or saying "well, let's see what they find?" Who would believe Cyber Ninja's results, given their CEO is a Trump supporter and conspiracy theorist? As Steller pointed out, how can their results be verified? How disturbing this mess has resulted from one person's Big Lie and that so many buy the lies. How fitting that a "Crazy Times" carnival was set up adjacent to the (unsecure) audit building. The carnival management should recruit Cyber Ninjas staff and AZ Senate Republicans for a new sideshow, "See the Loonies."

Published 5.23

TRUMP FAR FROM EXTRAORDINARY

Re: the June 4 letter "Onslaught against Trump never stops."

In a show of sympathy for Donald Trump the letter writer asks what your disposition would be if you experienced condemnation and scorn constantly. He says he has never witnessed such an onslaught on a president. Was he sleeping during the Obama administration?

Obama was called a Muslim, his status as a U.S. citizen constantly questioned, his wife compared to a man and an ape, and on and on. Obama ignored these and many other nasty smears with grace and intelligence. Trump, on the other hand, shows us just how unglued he truly is by his words, behavior, constant angry tweets, childish name calling and all of his other very unpresidential behavior. Extraordinary? That word usually carries a positive connotation, so I find it inappropriate to use it to describe Donald Trump.

Published 6.7

WHO NEEDS ENLIGHTENMENT?

Re: the July 12 letter "A primer for letter writers."

The letter intended to enlighten left-leaning contributors by simply listing six core beliefs of conservatives.

No. 3 on the list is not factual. America was not one of the first countries to eradicate slavery. Britain, Mexico, colonial Haiti and others beat us to it. (No mention of America's discrimination and "less than" treatment of descendants of slavery that continues to this day!)

No. 6 on the list was truly amazing -"We follow the science." (This put forth to delegitimize those identifying as transgender, who do not deny their birth gender.) If conservatives follow the science, why do so many dismiss the science surrounding COVID-19?

Donald Trump, many of his followers and many elected Republicans continue to deny, downplay and put out lies about the virus, vaccines and mask-wearing. Had science been followed, far fewer than 620,000 would have died. And let's not forget climate change denial. Following the science? Please do!

Published 7.14

RUDE, CRUDE, DEGRADING

Re: the Aug. 1 letter "More than unkind words."

The letter accuses some Star letter contributors of being "rude, crude, degrading" toward Republicans. Funny, those three words so aptly describe Donald Trump and many of his followers.

Trump unleashed a violent insurrection, openly denigrates women, and mocks handicapped people. His insurrectionists stormed the Capitol, assaulted Capitol police, and defecated in the halls. Yes, the GOP welcomes radicals with open arms – Marjorie Taylor Greene, Josh Hawley, Lauren Boebert, Jim Jordan – the list goes on within the GOP ranks.

We have the Proud Boys, Oath Keepers and many very angry MAGA folks who take part in or condone attacks on school boards, public health officials and the LGBTQ community. The GOP's own Rusty Bowers was treated to abhorrent harassment after telling the truth to the Jan. 6 committee. Vehicles with megaphones and signs proclaiming "pedophile" circled his house and made threats.

I am deeply offended by all the above. Just who is rude, crude and degrading?

DEMOCRACY ON THE BRINK

Re: the Aug. 3 article "Festival of democracy gone these days."

Trump supporters interviewed by Tim Steller at the polls expressed beliefs that because of Democrats the country is headed toward communism, socialism, and a host of other ills. One elderly couple stated they knew their votes in 2020 were not counted. How do they know this? Why, someone told them so!

A letter writer described these beliefs as "sad." Sad, yes – but it goes far beyond sad. It is frightening and dangerous that a significant number of seemingly otherwise intelligent people have, against all reason, bought the lies, misinformation and conspiracy theories set forth by Trump. They are unwavering in support of a twice-impeached, serial lying dictator wanna-be. They support the extremist candidates who bow to Trump, no matter that these extremists are set on destroying the fabric of our country.

Our democracy hangs on a precipice – not because of Democrats, but because Trump has succeeded in brainwashing and weaponizing gullible, easily led people who, like their cult leader, have no interest in truth or facts.

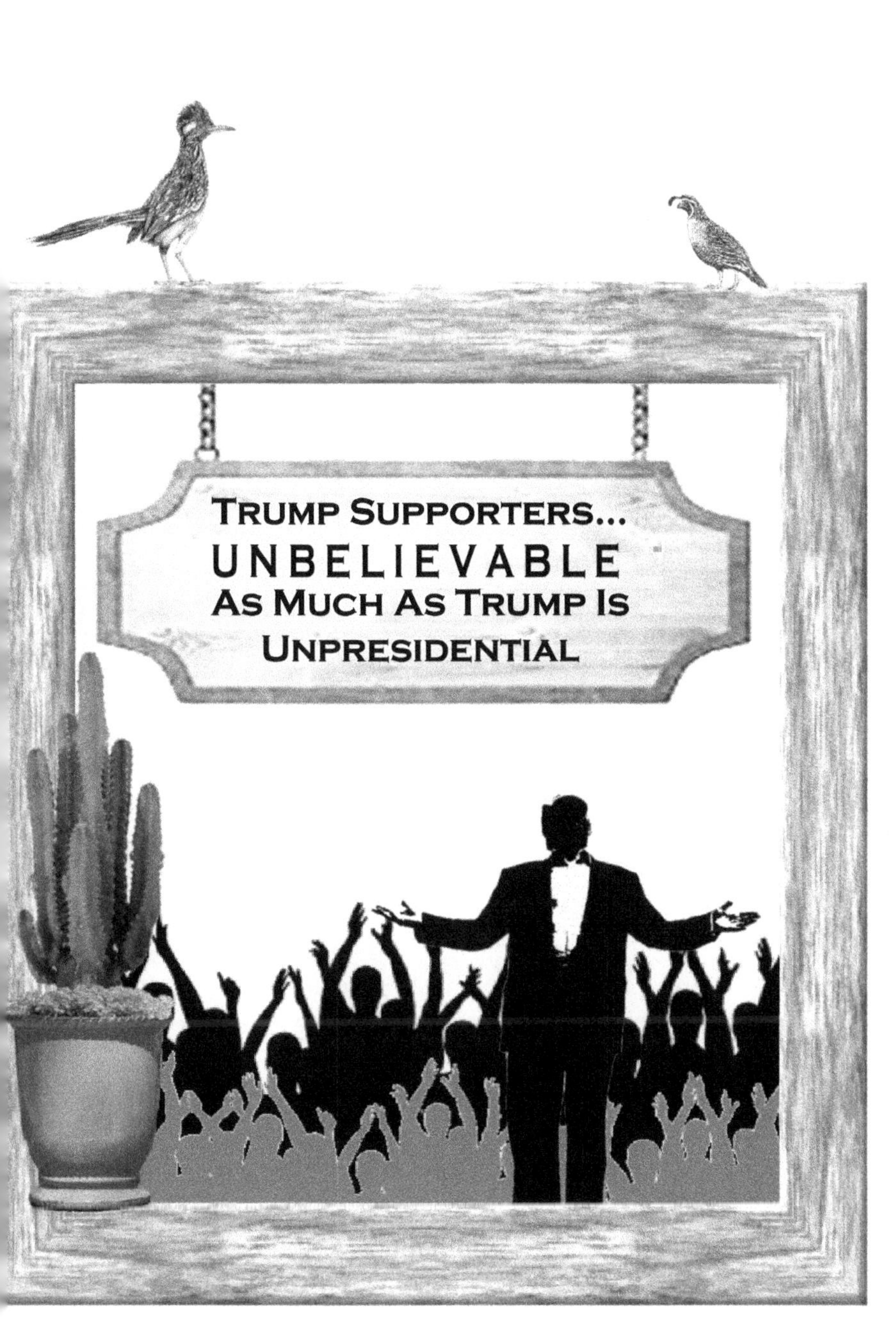
TRUMP SUPPORTERS...
UNBELIEVABLE
AS MUCH AS TRUMP IS
UNPRESIDENTIAL

CREEP-IN-CHIEF HAS NO PEER

The letter "Democrats' attacks are despicable" ended with calling Democratic senators "self-serving creeps." We have a president who disrespects and condones groping women. He publicly mocks victims of sexual assault. He uses the office of the president for his personal gain. Who is the self-serving creep?

WHAT'S NEXT, CHASTITY BELTS?

Someone tell me it's a joke. The Trump administration plans to spend many millions of Title IX federal grant money for family planning, giving preference to organizations that stress unrealistic abstinence and the rhythm method of birth control.

Study after study shows natural family planning to be very ineffective, with pregnancy resulting far more often than with science-based methods of contraception.

The ongoing attack on Planned Parenthood, women and science is ramping up. I knew it would be a short leap for Republicans to go from wanting to ban all abortions to banning contraception.

We're heading back to the Middle Ages. Maybe chastity belts can make a comeback under Trump. More jobs! But wait, they'd probably be made overseas.

CUSSING BAD, BUT GROPING IS OK?

I've read several letters carrying on about the terrible crime of cussing committed by Democratic politicians in recent days. Were these outraged letter writers offended by Donald Trump's groping of women, his describing it in derogatory, crude terms, and his unabashed bragging about it?

Did they write letters about that despicable behavior? That was criminal behavior, which certainly Trumps (pun intended) cussing when it comes to being inappropriate and crass.

NO PRESIDENTIAL PRAISE
FOR WAFFLE HOUSE HERO

Not one word of praise or the slightest accolade from the president for James Shaw Jr., the citizen who saved lives by stopping the Waffle House shooter in Nashville recently. One must wonder why. This hero ripped the AR-15 from the shooter and stopped a further massacre and was injured in the process.

Had this been accomplished by a white armed citizen, I'm sure we'd be hearing praises being sung far and wide. This scenario didn't fit into the 'good guys with guns' argument always touted by the right. The shooter will be undergoing mental health evaluation. Will anyone evaluate his ability to obtain assault weapons in the future? Probably not – we don't want to infringe on his Second Amendment rights, no matter what.

WHAT IF OBAMA HAD BEHAVED LIKE TRUMP?

What if President Obama had conducted himself, personally and professionally, like Donald Trump?. What if Obama had cozied up to Russian leader Vladimir Putin, knowing Russia meddled in our elections, and put on a performance like we witnessed in Helsinki? What if Obama unabashedly admitted paying off sexual partners, after first denying the affairs? Can you imagine the outrage, scathing criticism and calls for impeachment that would have erupted from Republicans? Yet they remain mostly silent – committed to coddling and protecting this treasonous, inept man who is destroying our democracy.

It is telling when conservative writer George Will speaks out as he did in "This sad, embarrassing wreck of a man" (July 19 edition of the Star). With great sadness, many of us watch what is happening to our country, the effects Trump's behavior and ineptitude are having here and throughout the world. Putin must be beyond ecstatic with his success in playing the POTUS like a fiddle. While Rome burns, Trump worries about kneeling football players.

-

A MEANINGLESS MEDAL

For those who like to write letters listing Donald Trump's accomplishments, add another to the list: making a total farce of the Presidential Medal of Freedom. Recipients given this award by Trump include right-wing radio talk show host and blabbermouth Rush Limbaugh, and now the obnoxious, ranting Jim Jordan of Ohio. Add on top of that another for devoted tattler and Trump sycophant Devin Nunes.

Who next? Michel Flynn? Paul Manafort? Jon Voight? The "My Pillow" guy? Kiss Donald's ring and you shall be rewarded! What an insult to past, legitimate, deserving recipients of the once-honorable award. It's forever tainted and now rendered meaningless.

COINCIDENCE OR CORRUPTION?

A recent letter wants us to believe that Postmaster General Louis DeJoy's appointment had nothing to do with being a big Trump donor/supporter. A letter writer says that's irrelevant. It's not irrelevant, it's corrupt.

Are we really supposed to believe that someone with no experience in our postal service was the most qualified candidate among dozens of others with many years of postal service experience? Please. We're not stupid or deluded.

How uncanny that DeJoy just happens to be a Trump donor/supporter! How convenient that he's now in charge of the post office, already carrying out the plans to suppress vote-by-mail, though that is being totally denied. Maybe the "My Pillow" guy, another Trump supporter who was indicted in California for making false claims about his products, will get the next important position that opens up during this administration's quest to destroy and remake our government. He claims to have a COVID-19 cure; will he be the newest addition to the Trump world?

FOOL ME TWICE,
AND TRUMP'S ELECTION IS ON YOU

A recent letter writer shared his displeasure with Fitz's cartoons, finding them insulting to the president. I wonder if he also finds the president's frequent nasty insults he hurls at anyone he dislikes or that doesn't agree with him offensive? Or is that Ok?

It is way past time to bring common decency and integrity back to the White House. We've had enough of rudeness, bullying, nastiness, ineptitude, total chaos and disregard for the rule of law and the norms of our democracy. I've voted for decency.

If the country wants more of reality TV "governing" and the continuation of the dangerous dismantling of our democracy by electing the current clown yet again, the saying, "people get the government they deserve" will come into play. One time, a sad and devastating mistake. Twice – incomprehensible and quite possibly the end of our democracy.

TRUTH SERUM?

What a surprise! Donald Trump, in his bizarre and insultingly inappropriate Memorial Day tweet, so accurately described a faction of his own supporters (and himself). He called out "terrorists, misfits, lunatic thugs, communists, Marxists and fascist pigs." Donald Trump, I'm amazed. I never thought you'd be so truthful. Are you finally looking at the truth of Jan. 6? And saying our nation has never been in greater peril, right on. I am astounded at your newfound insights. What gives?

May 2023

BIBLE-SIGNING STUNT
THE ULTIMATE FARCE

Re: "Some Religious leaders say they have no problem with Trump signing Bibles."

Donald Trump — serial liar, adulterer, predatory capitalist and Russian collaborator — signing Bibles in Alabama.

The hypocrisy meter is exploding. This is the ultimate political stunt.

Who came up with this idea? I think I know. No doubt he equates this to an author's book signing. Ponder the pomposity and absurdity of this stunt. Who would want to take part in such a farce?

If Trump exemplifies Christian values and teaching, the so-called Christians who would covet his Bible signature should re-examine their religion and try to determine how it so egregiously ran off the rails.

OBVIOUS THAT
TRUMP IS PUTIN'S STOOGE

What a circus show we are witnessing, with Donald Trump, Rudy Giuliani, Bill Barr and Co. It's not a sideshow but the main act going on nonstop under the big top of GOP corruption. The lying, denying, spinning, and smearing escalating as the corrupter in chief exploded in rage after releasing his self-damning "perfect" extortion phone call to Ukraine's president.

Flying-monkey Giuliani is sparring with the corrupt attorney general, while the high priest of corruption brings Pence into the fray. No one could make this stuff up, and it's tremendously scary to think this is the low to which our country has devolved. The article "For help with Ukraine, Giuliani turned to unlikely pair of fixers from Florida" shows just how the Republicans operate.

It is so obvious Trump is Vladimir Putin's stooge. Republican sycophants in Congress continue to rally around Trump, folding to their fear of losing elections if they dare speak out against Trump's treasonous behavior. Cowards all!

HOW DO YOU SPELL RELIEF?
NO MORE TRUMP

The bully child in the White House is throwing a huge tantrum, very unhappy he lost the election. Some adults (if there are any) need to grab the toddler and paddle his rear end till he can't sit down. Timeouts will not work.

Miscreant "leader" Donald Trump tried mightily and is still trying, to create mistrust in our voting system with his lies of voter and vote-counting fraud. He shamefully engaged in massive voter suppression attempts, but the American people persevered despite post office changes, fewer polling places, fewer drop box locations and a pandemic. They rejected the last four years of bullying, nastiness, corruption, ineptitude and deadly mishandling of a public health crisis.

What a relief to think about having a mature, competent, empathetic person in the White House – one that wants to unite not divide; one who pledges to be a president for all Americans. How will we act without the daily chaos?

GIVE CREDIT WHERE CREDIT IS DUE

A recent letter accused Sen. Jeff Flake of destroying "the well-being of the country" via his animosity toward the president.

Let's give proper credit where credit is due. There is only one person responsible for the ruination of our democracy and destruction of the country's well-being, and that is Donald J Trump.

RESPECT

HAIL TO STORMY!

There once was a woman named Stormy,
who meets an ex-prez who was horny

She started to squeal on the arrogant heel
He then denied date-night with Stormy

Then Michael the lawyer did pay
To keep troublesome Stormy at bay

To prison he went, his loyalty spent
All Hail, All Hail to Stormy!

IT WORKS BOTH WAYS

Re: the Jan. 2 letter "Poor planning."

I agree with the letter so far as pregnancies should be planned, every child should be wanted and parents able to afford and adequately provide for the child. Men bear equal responsibility in the decision making.

However, an abortion should be an option for those who didn't plan or who for various reasons decide against a pregnancy . The letter gets silly in speculating the loss of future presidents, doctors and soldiers via abortion. I can think of several political figures who would have left the world a better place by leaving it at the zygote stage. In following the letter writer's thinking, abortion could possibly spare us another Hitler, another Putin, another Jeffrey Dahmer, or another chaos-creating megalomaniac politician. But the bottom line is all women should have control over their own bodies and safe access to abortion if that is their choice.

RESPECT MUST BE EARNED

Re: the Jan. 10 letter to the editor "Showing respect for the president."

The letter claimed that just because you dislike the president doesn't mean you can disrespect him. In other words, one must respect the president no matter what.

I always believed in the premise that respect must be earned. Anyone can foster disrespect by their actions, words or behavior – whether president or common citizen. No one can command or demand respect. It is not an inherent given for any position or title.

In the case of the POTUS, who himself is probably among the top three most disrespectful people on earth, there has been little show of respect- worthy behavior.

I see no criteria for respect in his continual lying, bullying behavior, demeaning attitude and actions towards women, pomposity and arrogance, and name-calling and denigration of anyone who disagrees with him. Respectful people generally garner respect. Trump has earned any disrespect that has come his way; no one can decree he be respected because he happens to be the president. It doesn't work that way.

Published January 15

BE SURE TO WEAR SOME
FLOWERS IN YOUR HAIR

Re: the Feb 2 letter to the editor "Flower children made their bed."

The letter casts a wide net, blaming the flower child generation for a host of societal ills. The number of societal crimes that conservatives of that time (known then as the Establishment) can take credit for would fill pages – including an immoral war that took the lives of 58,209 Americans. If not for the protests of my generation, we might still be in that unwinnable war. The divide persists today.

My moral compass much prefers association with the flower children than with their counterparts, who today walk around in MAGA hats and still think Vietnam was a good idea. I'm thankful to have been on the side of peace, equality and nonviolence. No regrets or complaints – I'm happy to pay property taxes, don't have children, and manage OK with Social Security.

Amazing that there are people out there still wanting to trash the generation that changed the nation and played a big part in ending a useless war. "Peace."

Published February 15

INSANITY RULES

Arizona has gone down Insanity Lane. The Big Lie continues to flourish. Drag queens are Public Enemy No. 1. Parents can carry guns onto school property and are considered more expert than educators about the curriculum. Books are banned. There's a new hotline for reporting teachers suspected of teaching that favorite Republican culture war topic, critical race theory. No worries about false accusations against teachers, says State Superintendent of Public Instruction Tom Horne. According to him, his legal background will enable him to ferret out wrongful accusations. This reassurance should have prospective teachers waiting in line to apply. Next on the list, book burning? I think I smell gasoline and matches being lit. I hope kids will follow the advice of author Stephen King and run to the nearest library or bookstore and find out what they're not supposed to be reading. Or will bookstores and libraries be banned? These Republican extremists like to throw out words like "Marxist", "socialist," "groomers", "woke." Given what they are doing, the term "Nazi-like" is appropriate.

Published March 16

RESPONSE FROM READER RECEIVED IN THE MAIL: 3/16 Thank you for your letter to the editor I always look forward to reading your contributions. *Insanity rules,* indeed!

KIND OF A DRAG

Republicans, you must be so proud your chosen legislators have prioritized attacking Public Enemy No. 1 – drag queens. Justine Wadsack leads the charge in Arizona. (Having observed Justine's pre-election shenanigans and now this, I find her to be rather scary, and I don't think I'd want a child around her.)   This attack on drag and LGBTQ in general is a Republican culture war tactic designed to rile the base nationwide. It's very popular and successful. I wonder, do these Republican drag-phobes worry about children seeing the violent video from Jan 6th? A crazed mob attacking and maiming police, setting up gallows ("Hang Mike Pence! Hang Mike Pence! USA USA!"), desecration of the capitol, and bloodthirsty mobs going after Congressional members. Surely more harmful to kids than exposure to drag. Oh wait, I forgot! Those violent insurrectionists are great patriots, their violence that day admirable! No doubt   Tucker Carlson is working on spinning all that video gifted him by Kevin McCarthy into the Republican fairy tale version. Stay tuned.

THE MOTHER
OF ALL DENIGRATORS

Re: the June 17 article "Numbing bureaucrats invite backlash."

John Kass takes great offense to the term "birthing person" being used instead of "mother" in federal and scientific documents. He thinks this denigrates and disparages "the essence of motherhood and women." Seriously? I found Donald Trump's disparaging of women and mothers far more offensive than the words "birthing person." Kass suggests Americans will push back for the egregious use of the words "birthing person" in documents. The American people have already pushed back – in November 2020 – by voting out a rude, crude incompetent who also denigrates women.

COVID

A LITTLE RHYME TO PASS THE TIME

I wear a mask and hold my breath

One might think I'm scared to death

If other humans come too near

I quickly move away in fear

Our lives have really changed a lot

You might have it, you might not

There's really no good way to know

With testing numbers very low

The Chosen One said it's a hoax

As sickness spreads among the folks

Think he cares 'bout You? Heck no

He cares for his portfolio!

SUDDEN EMBRACE OF COVID SCIENCE

Those who could get vaccinated but choose not to, should not get priority treatment for hospital care or ICU beds. Why should others needing care or surgery take a back seat or have to postpone procedures because of the irresponsible choice of others?

Funny how those who denied and refused the science pertaining to COVID before falling ill are suddenly very happy – even desperate - to embrace science from their hospital beds.

Prior to being hospitalized with the virus, how often did they think about the stress and strain on the hospital staff they now depend upon for their very lives?

Insurance companies must be fine with paying out huge sums for the medical care of people too obstinate or ignorant to take advantage of the vaccines. Insurers should wise up – no vaccine, no hospital coverage. Maybe that would help stop the stupidity.

A NEW LOW

I recall standing in line at my elementary school in Ohio to receive the polio vaccine. There were no protesters outside; no angry, loud parents making threats or carrying zip ties or creating a ruckus. By everyone cooperating with what was needed for the common good, polio was eradicated in the U.S.A.

What has happened to our once-civilized country? Recently I saw a vehicle flying a huge flag displaying the most profane, derogatory two-word statement for our current president. Four years of a mouthy, derisive, belligerent and hatefully disrespectful miscreant has made such behavior acceptable and commonplace. Trump encouraged and emboldened the worst among us, and their behavior easily segues into violence as we saw happen Jan. 6.

Unlike people in the days of polio, many are willing to expose themselves and others to a deadly virus to make some kind of political statement. How sad our country has devolved to such a low place.

PLACE BLAME WHERE IT BELONGS

There's been a plethora of articles and letters blaming Biden for the troubling state of COVID in America. Really? Biden has, from Day 1, begged Americans to get vaccinated – the key to ending this miserable pandemic. Most of the blame belongs on those who refuse vaccination and won't follow experts' recommendations for masking and social distancing. They are the ones spreading the mutating virus and creating a huge strain on our hospitals and medical staff.

Also deserving blame are spreaders of misinformation, lies and false theories about the virus, suggesting quack "cures" or unproven alternative remedies. This includes the former president and some of his supporters in Washington. These same people discredit and denigrate medical experts, further fueling vaccine hesitancy. Some letters ignorantly spout the fact of more COVID deaths under Biden than under Trump, as if that somehow proves Biden is responsible. I believe more deaths are the result of obstinate refusal of some to consider the public good, with no concern about spreading a deadly virus. Who really is to blame?

GOP PRO-COVID
SO IT CAN BLAME BIDEN

Plain and simple, the Republican Party is pro-COVID. Hyping of unapproved drugs and dangerous "cures" (ingest cleaning chemicals), there is no inkling of sanity showing from the Party of Death.

Republican governors have banned mask mandates for schools, willing to sacrifice your kids to show allegiance to Trump. Shameful attacks on public workers and school employees are tolerated. Being pro-COVID will keep the economy from recovering . I think that is their plan. Then blame Biden.

In his recent speech about fighting COVID, our president said "patience is wearing thin" with those resisting vaccination. Former Vice President Mike Pence took great offense, claiming those words were highly inappropriate. This from the guy who was OK with Donald Trump's words commanding his supporters on Jan 6 to storm the Capitol, with the murder of Mike Pence on their "to do" list. Incredible.

MUCH HARDSHIP WAS PREVENTABLE

Re: the Jan. 28 "A tired Tucson becomes careless."

Yes, it would be great to have some official in every store or venue to enforce public health safety measures. Not gonna happen. Many stores have no mask policy anymore. We have a pro-COVID governor fighting public safety measures tooth and nail. I recently had to enter a drugstore, glad to see a "mask required" sign. I saw a woman have a coughing spell while checking out, pulling her mask away from her face. Seriously? Then I saw a delivery guy walk through the store unmasked. All the while, the store's public service announcement about masking and social distancing was playing. The experience totally reinforced why I make as few trips into stores as possible. Ultimately, it is up to each individual to make choices for the public good; however, many refuse to cooperate and/or just don't take COVID seriously. That's why we are entering Year 3 of this pandemic with all of its limitations, hardships, ongoing illness and unnecessary deaths.

FACTS OVER NONSENSE

Re: the Feb 4 letter "Time to accept COVID-19 reality."

This letter showed a complete lack of knowledge about the virus. It also displays the "me" mindset that the unvaccinated need only be concerned about their own situation. The author suggested those infected with COVID who have minor, or no symptoms, really aren't sick, and therefore don't have a real case of COVID. In other words, if you have no significant symptoms, it doesn't exist – an ignorant and dangerous belief! Never mind that asymptomatic people can spread the virus. To suggest the medical community is using these 'non-cases' to inflate COVID numbers is ludicrous. The letter ends saying the government should focus on providing resources to handle COVID issues, rather than push vaccination. The government is doing both. Some conservative-leaning places are refusing financial help, like Cochise County, where the Board of Supervisors recently turned down $1.9 million in COVID relief funds. Brilliant! Those supervisors who voted "no" probably agree with the nonsense presented in this letter.

MANY MAKING WRONG CHOICES

Re: the Feb. 14 letter "Value of freedom eludes leaders."

The letter left me wondering what reality the author is living in. The American people have been given all the necessary education about the virus and vaccines. This information has been dispersed by scientists, medical experts, public-health officials and responsible government officials. Certain mandates came into play when it became obvious that many informed "proud Americans" are not choosing to do the right thing, refusing to heed science and common sense. According to the letter, if people are just given their "freedom," they will make the correct choice, as the country did during the polio epidemic. This is a totally different time, where people actually think social media is a legitimate source of information and many have bought into the politicization of this pandemic. Right-wing politicians continue to sow doubt and distrust in science and facts surrounding COVID-19 and vaccines. Some Americans are doing the right thing, but many are not. Having no mandates and therefore "freedom," would not change this.

MASK REFUSAL INSULTS VETERANS

Re: the May 31 article "Dear Dad, thinking of you today."

I enjoyed Sara Hammond's Memorial Day tribute to her father.

It made me think of my own father, overseas in the South Pacific; Mom was home with a baby. Mom didn't drive, and things had to be difficult. I thought of my husband's father flying 88 missions in a P-47 Thunderbolt.

And people think wearing a mask is a huge sacrifice and has something to do with their freedom! I think about those individuals in our government now, entrusted to keep our democracy strong, who are doing all they can to destroy it with their voter suppression efforts and their complete disregard for truth and facts.

They are willing to perpetrate a lie and destroy trust in future elections to maintain power and show allegiance to a wannabe dictator. They whitewash a violent attack on the Capitol by Donald Trump supporters. They are willing to destroy our democracy without thinking twice about it. Is this what our veterans sacrificed for? Shameful!

DUMB IS FOREVER

Re: the July 19 letter "There's no chip in your arm."

A recent letter explained how government-implanted microchips (if such a thing existed) would be too large to pass through a vaccination needle. The hope being the segment of our population who actually believe the microchip conspiracy will accept truth and science and possibly go get vaccinated. What do you think the chances of that are? As Judge Judy has told us, "Beauty fades, dumb is forever."

The latest pandemic surge is just beginning. We can thank Republican downplaying of the virus, ridiculous messaging about personal freedom, and refusal to call for masking, vaccination and other mitigation measures.   Their callousness toward vulnerable children, the immunocompromised and others at risk who cannot be vaccinated is appalling, as is their lack of concern for health care and other front-line workers. The stalwart elephant is no longer a fitting symbol for the GOP, a new logo is needed. How about replacing the pachyderm with a large COVID-19 virus? That would be appropriate.

WANT SCHOOLS OPEN?
JOIN THE FRONT LINES

It's plain to see – teachers are the new punching bags. I've read numerous letters saying kids and teachers need to get back to school, citing meaningless statistics (child deaths from car accidents, isolated flu cases – hardly preventable). COVID deaths are preventable. No child or school employee should be put at risk.

One callous letter took the "collateral damage" stance – yes, it will be tragic, but some must die to keep our schools open! The same letter cited Asian and European schools opening, ignoring the fact that most other countries, unlike ours, have successfully curtailed this virus.   Another letter suggested teachers felt privileged, wanting to stay home with pay, suggesting it's a teacher's job to "care for children."

No, that's a parent's job. If you feel so strongly that schools be open despite the risk, then go volunteer several days a week in the schools, helping those entitled teachers monitor and enforce the kids' mask-wearing, social distancing and hygiene measures – up close and personal.

NOT YOUR RIGHT TO MAKE OTHERS SICK

Re: the August 25 letter "Attacks on those who are not vaccinated."

There have been several letters comparing the unvaccinated to those who might be harming themselves by being obese, by smoking or engaging in other self-destructive behaviors. The key concept here is self-destructive.

Being obese harms only the overweight person. Serious health issues from smoking mainly harm the smoker. This cannot in any way be legitimately compared to the spreading of a highly infectious virus that could leave others gravely ill, or dead.

Can those who think their unvaccinated status poses no threat to others really be that dense? I find that hard to believe. They simply think they can do as they please without regard for others, including children and those with underlying health issues who are at high risk.

This mindset is the height of self-centered and callous disregard for others. Yes, it's your body but when your decisions can cause illness and death to others and you just don't care, that says a lot about you.

FORGOTTEN GROUP IN 'ROLL CALL'

Re: the Sept. 12 letter "Roll call for the unvaccinated."

The letter provided a list of groups who are resisting vaccination, and the reasons why. Pretty accurate, but one significant group was left out- those with a political axe to grind. Many are still embracing the original words and messaging of Donald Trump –"it's a hoax, it will disappear, it's like the flu, kids don't get it " etc.

As did Trump, some conservatives are still promoting quack cures, and ineffective drugs (horse de-wormer, anyone?). Though the ex-president is now saying "Take the vaccine," his prior words and messaging have done a great disservice to public health and have done much to keep this pandemic alive and well. How unfortunate many still buy into that dangerous and false messaging, keeping us from vanquishing the virus and getting back to some degree of normalcy.

WHAT THE DIFFERENCE REALLY IS

Re: the Oct 2 article "Unvaxxed couple tells of COVID-19's ferocity."

Kudos to Patty Machelor for the story on the Tucson couple's frightening battle with COVID-19. Kudos also to the Masons for sharing their story. As the article pointed out, many people with vaccine hesitancy have expressed the belief that "there is something different" about this new vaccine that makes them leery of it. This despite the fact they have embraced many other vaccines, flu shots, pneumonia shots, etc. and that there is plenty of scientific proof that the vaccine is safe and very effective. What makes people think this vaccine is "different?" The belief in "different" stems from Republicans, including ex-president Trump, sowing and nurturing distrust of the vaccine, encouraging conspiracy theories and spreading gross misinformation about COVID and the vaccine. (Never mind that most of them quietly got vaccinated) . It stems from not doing your own fact-finding from credible sources.   That is the difference, tragically a very dangerous and in many cases, deadly difference.

BIDEN TIME

WHO'S THE GENIUS?

Re: the May 2 letter "Say no to ethanol."

The author says that President Biden will be to blame for wrecking fuel systems in millions of vehicles. The reasoning? Some car manufacturers recommend not using fuel containing more than 10% ethanol. Wouldn't it be up to the vehicle owners to read their manual and know what type of fuel to use? But if you can blame Biden for any negative outcome resulting from your own irresponsibility, why not?

And speaking of "genius in the White House," recall the last "very stable genius" who suggested we might ingest or inject cleaning chemicals to combat the COVID-19 virus and who floated the idea of detonating a nuclear bomb in the eye of hurricanes to mitigate a storm's power. Donald Trump bragged about how he aced some sort of mental acuity test, where he was able to identify a rhinoceros, a lion, and a camel (clear proof of genius). He also can claim bragging rights to destruction of a democracy more than 200 years old.

WHO'S THE TRAITOR?

Re: the May 21 letter "USA, Third World Country?"

Without offering an opinion of any reasons or justifications, the letter claimed President Joe Biden and his administration are "deliberately destroying the USA and should be tried for treason for betraying oath of office to uphold the Constitution." I can think of no one more treasonous or guilty of such betrayal of office than Donald Trump. What does the letter writer think should be the proper punishment for Trump for telling Georgia Secretary of State Raffensperger to find 11,780 votes (this on tape)? What punishment fits for inciting a deadly insurrection for the purpose of overturning a free and fair election? Talk about treason! What should happen to a person who has worked nonstop to destroy our election system by telling lies over and over about election fraud? What about being Vladimir Putin's very useful and willing idiot (recall Helsinki)? Insert "Trump" wherever "Biden" appears in the letter, and you have something that makes sense.

MONSTER WON'T GO AWAY

Donald Trump is so frustrated and jealous of Joe Biden's successful handling of COVID-19. His response is to renew his attacks on Dr. Fauci, and his minions are following his lead. How ridiculous that this guy who was touting ingesting or injecting chemicals and pushing a drug known to be ineffective against the virus is continuing to denigrate one of the world's foremost virus experts.

His sycophant supporters like Sen. Ron Johnson of Wisconsin and Sen. Rand Paul of Kentucky are joining in. Sen. Johnson recently tried to give new life to the hydroxychloroquine falsehood. Recall, early on, Trump publicly expressed his jealousy (in a joking way, but he was obviously not joking) that Dr. Fauci was more popular than Trump when Fauci was part of Trump's virus team.

Shortly after that, Dr. Fauci was muzzled and all but disappeared. Now he must have a security detail to protect him and his family. What a sad commentary on Trump and his followers.

Published 6.21

WITH TRUMP, THERE'S NO BOTTOM

Re: the Nov 11 article "Although election has come to an end, GOP's bad faith lives on."

Michael Gersen did a spectacular job with this opinion piece. I can't imagine a better explanation of the deep, depraved depths to which Donald Trump and his Republican enablers have sunk, post-election.

Just when you think they can't possibly go any lower, you're proven wrong once again. Besides showing themselves as total fools, their shameful, despicable attempt to subvert our election process – our very democracy – will be one for the history books. Stay tuned, they are not yet done.

Published 11.26

TRUMP HAS NOT EARNED
THE RESPECT OF VOTERS

Re: the Nov 21 letter "Let voters make final judgment on president."

I read this with incredulity; another Trump supporter who thinks just because a person is president, he or she deserves respect regardless of actions or behavior. The letter writer is so worried by how our youth might be affected by people not respecting the president. I ask, how are youth being affected by the president's continual lying, nasty bullying behavior and disrespectful language? Just last week, he called a member of Congress "human scum."

Add in his adulterous affairs, corruption and abuse of office that is being exposed in the impeachment hearings. There are many youth who are tuned into what is going on. As they see the president in action and the truth coming out, are they thinking this is all OK? Obviously the letter writer does. Sorry, respect is to be earned and this president has earned as much respect as he shows to others and to the office of the president (zero).

Published 12.9

WHO CARES?

A recent letter told us that President Joe Biden and the Democratic Party care zero about the "little people."   The supposition must follow that it's Republicans who do care. I cannot stop laughing.

How many of you little people have benefitted from the huge tax cuts for the super-wealthy and big corporations?   Has your family benefited from climate change denials, public school defunding, from voter suppression measures?   Republicans don't want you voting unless it is for them.

Women, do you like Republicans decreeing you must give birth, even if raped? How caring! Who benefited from the lies and misinformation spread about COVID? Maybe some of you lost loves ones in part due to this misinformation and science denial. Republicans vowed to destroy President Barack Obama's Affordable Care Act, which provided me affordable health insurance prior to Medicare. Thank you, Democrats!

Let's hear from all the little people who feel Republicans truly care about us. I doubt the Star will need to hire extra staff to handle the influx of testimonials.

GUNS

HOW DOES
KILLING VENERATE NATURE?

Re: the Oct 24 article "Mixed reaction to proposed plan for Ironwood recreational shooting."

I fail to see how destroying nature would help anyone "get close to nature." Hiking, yes. Birding, yes. Nature photography, yes. Maiming, hurting and killing nature's creatures? How that would be enjoyable to anyone is mind-boggling. It smacks of disrespect, lack of compassion and indifference to other living things.

Besides destroying animals in their habitat, the destruction to that habitat and to petroglyphs should not be allowed. Add to that the noise pollution and danger to others using the areas.

Given the popularity and acceptance of this cruel and violent pastime, it's no big surprise that our country's frequent mass shootings of people are forgotten after several days.

TAKING THE PRIZE

Re: the Dec 3 letter "A modest proposal."

After reading this letter several times, I came to the realization that this letter wasn't sick sarcasm or an unfunny joke, but that the author was deadly serious.   Incredibly, she proposed a day of recognition for those innocents murdered by gun violence, to show our thanks and appreciation for taking a bullet so that the rest of us can enjoy our Second Amendment rights to be able to "protect ourselves."   I guess the right to life, liberty and pursuit of happiness of those murdered takes a backseat to others' gun rights. But aren't we good, appreciative people? Let's honor those who have had their lives snuffed out by disturbed gun nuts, so we can continue our gun idolatry. A national day of recognition, the least we can do! This letter takes the prize for most outrageous opinion to grace the pages of the Star and serves as a frightening glimpse into the mindset of gun worship.

NOT CUTE

The photo of Sen. Justine Wadsack and Rep. Rachel Jones posing in high heels, holding guns in front of the old state capitol building is pathetic. They obviously think they're cute. What an embarrassment to be represented in LD17 by these two and the rest of "the freedom team". Who voted for these people?

GOP GUNS OVER PEOPLE

Another horrific mass shooting of little kids and school employees in the land of gun worship where human life is less valuable than your right to have guns. There is much talk of mental health, as if that somehow negates easy access to weapons and our sick, gun-glorifying culture. Republican Barry Moore of Alabama along with George Santos and Lauren Boebert, are proposing a bill to make the AR-15 our "national gun." Sheer lunacy.

What next, mass shooters memorialized on a Mount Rushmore-type monument? Some in Congress are sporting AR-15 label pins, a nice touch. My favorite, the Christmas cards of politicians' families, smiling holding their assault rifles around the Christmas tree. Just what is the message there? Would these gun fetishists choose another holiday greeting or a different lapel pin if their child became a victim of gun violence? What is wrong with these people? Why would anyone vote for someone who values unrestricted gun access over a child's life? Talk about questionable mental health!

ADS A BAROMETER OF DECENCY

In a famous 1954 hearing, lawyer Joseph Welch asked Sen. Joseph McCarthy "at long last, have you left no sense of decency?" The same question could be posed to Republican candidates running ads showing themselves using, holding and firing assault and other weapons. We saw Jim Lamon in a Wild West shootout, firing at Biden, Pelosi, and Mark Kelley. There's Karrin Robson and Blake Masters shooting and glorifying assault weapons of carnage. My personal favorite – Jerone Davison - a Black candidate shown leveling his AR at a group of supposed Democrats coming for him, dressed in full KKK garb. After all the recent and past gun violence, the heartbreaking testimony of children who survived Uvalde, what kind of person could possibly think these gun-glorifying violence-endorsing ads are OK? They are despicable. I think these ads show that the candidates they represent are depraved, incredibly callous and truly devoid of decency.

ALL KINDS OF SEWAGE

Re: the Dec. 16 letter "Sonoran sewage around the clock."

I admit I also took note of the heavy coverage given the Sonoran sewage problem. But, it is important. I'm not sure what the holiday season should have to do with reporting disturbing news. Choosing what news you want is like choosing what history you want. The letter said, "in America we are trying to bring good news to the country." Well, that would be very nice, and the more good news the better, but a lot of America's news is far worse than the sewage story – an attempted election coup, a deadly insurrection on Jan. 6, an ongoing deadly virus that is being politicized and yet another school massacre by a disturbed 15-year-old whose parents gifted him the weapon. Think the parents of the murdered and wounded kids are feeling like celebrating America and the joyous Christmas season? If you put on your dark rose-colored glasses, you might be able to ignore sewage, Sonoran or other varieties.

EDUCATION

TROUBLE FOR AZ SCHOOLS

Like the Creature from the Black Lagoon, Tom Horne has emerged from the muck again to head up Arizona schools. His right wing "vision" for education is appalling. Who voted for this guy? Do parents really buy the critical race theory baloney? Voters rejected most of the other extremists on the ballot, what happened here? His opponent should be demanding an investigation, a la sore loser Republicans.

STATE'S EDUCATION
AD IS LIPSTICK ON A PIG

Re: the Jan. 31 letter to the editor "Rankings don't tell the whole story."

It's probably safe to assume the letter writer is fine with the appalling teacher compensation in Arizona. I guess this falls under his "better results for less cost" argument. All Arizonans should be ashamed of an education system that pays teachers about the same as someone in a job requiring no education or special skills. Expecting that our teachers be fairly compensated is not a liberal mind-set.

How about using most of the ad campaign money for teacher compensation and on improving the schools? I doubt the ad campaign is going to convince anyone that things are hunky-dory with regard to Arizona schools. What a waste of funds to put lipstick on a pig!

WHO REALLY WANTS TO INDOCTRINATE?

Re: the June 3 article "Brainwashing claims are distracting from school funding issues."

Many thanks to Heather Mace for her opinion piece. I, too, was struck by the outrageous claims put forth by the Republican candidates for superintendent of public instruction in the voter education guide. Accusations of student indoctrination with "liberal propaganda," brainwashing, CRT, woke agenda and other total nonsense were in the bios of each Republican candidate. Typical right-wing, anti-public-school garbage. It's amazing that highly educated people would stoop to this. I think these people are anti-public education and want our tax dollars taken from public schools and awarded to schools where the students really will be indoctrinated in right-wing ideology and revisionist history. Two words for this anti-public education, anti-teacher effort: beyond disgusting. Do not vote for those who work to erode our public schools. Interesting to note, the voter guide was put out by Citizens Clean Election Commission – the very name falsely implying that past elections were somehow not legitimate.

VOUCHER INSANITY

Any family can get a $7K school voucher handout, per child, at the expense of our public schools and you, the taxpayer. Private schools are not accountable for any reporting – financial or educational – the way public schools are. Parents receiving these funds can use them any way they please, supposedly to be used for alternative educational needs. Republicans keep harping on importance of school "choice." (How ironic that concept of choice doesn't apply to women's reproductive rights.)

Financial need is not a requirement to receive the voucher funds. No wonder the projection is for 943 million to be spent on this ill-conceived Republican giveaway. The latest report shows 53% of K-12 spending will go to just 8% of Arizona students. And people are OK with this? The public schools must beg our communities to donate school supplies, this plea is repeated over and over on the local news every morning. Fully funding our public schools should come first. Something is very wrong here!

Published August 8, 2023

KARI

CALLING OUT CINOs

Re: the Sept. 24 article "Kari Lake's Christ is unfamiliar to this heathen sinner."

Kudos to Fitz for his article shining a spotlight on these phony CINOs (Christians in name only). What could be more repugnant than these Republican politicians, including Donald Trump, masquerading as Godly people to pander to evangelical voters? What a farce. I wonder if the MAGA evangelicals have ever taken notice of the perfect description of their earthly orange Messiah set forth in Proverbs 6:12 – 19, "The Wicked Man." Absolutely spot on accurate.

KARI ALIENATED TOO MANY

Brilliant move by Kari Lake to alienate many moderate Republican voters with her nasty remarks and gestures towards John McCain and those who respect what he stood for. Her exaggerated "drive a stake through the heart" theater was the epitome of classlessness. Maybe some local theater groups desperate for actors and willing to train will be reaching out to Kari. Like Trump, when before an audience, she feels the need to throw out red meat that gets the easily manipulated base all riled up. Is she at all embarrassed by that despicable, childish display? Of course not! If you had any doubts Kari does not possess "the right stuff," that act should make it crystal clear.

Published 12.15

MISC.

ON POPULATION THINK SMALLER

Re: Jan 3 article "US would be more happy with more people."

This piece ranks in the top three most absurd articles I've read in the Star's opinion pages in several years. Tyler Cowen claims America is in a funk, needing more people to achieve "momentum" and "ascending successes" to push us toward "successively stronger positions" (whatever those are). Then the clincher – the more patriotic among us realize we need a larger populace. Cowen must support totally open borders, a quick way to achieve his wish to grow America's population. Much faster than procreation. He tells us how much more exciting he finds cities and states with lots of people. To each his own, I guess. At what point might the realization dawn that more people might not be a desirable thing? Environmental issues? Not to worry, according to Cowen, more people translates into more chances to solve our dire climate crisis. You know, that planet-threatening crisis caused by too many people and their irresponsible handling of "ascending successes."

BACK TO THE CLOSET

Re: the June 26 letter "Don't beg for trouble." It seems the premise of the letter is that LGBTQs should fade into the woodwork. The letter suggests "doing your own thing in daily life without drama."   Just maybe, the long history of ostracization, discrimination, hate and violence towards LGBTQs has created a desire for some to "put it out there".   Somehow loud displays and theatrics are ok for heterosexuals – think Super Bowl halftime, St. Patrick's Day, Mardi Gras, Trump rallies and other over the top events. Reading the letter, I got the feeling that LGBTQs, even if friends and family, are still "the other". "We've come to love and accept them". (It wasn't unconditional from the get-go).   "They have proven to be intelligent, creative and productive citizens". (They had to prove it!) And, they have to "win us over" by not being flamboyant and in-your-face – "Being obnoxious creates few supporters" (Unless you are Donald Trump). The overall message – LGBTQs, be grateful – you are finally gaining some acceptance, so behave yourselves!

**ALL OVER THE NATION –
MISINFORMATION**

So COVID-19 was a hoax
Why so many dying folks?
Donald Trump – hey, he won!
His cult, each and every one
Thinks it's true, wear your red,
 white and blue
Jan. 6, just another normal day!
The dead and maimed, what to say?
So many lies, so much at stake
Ask Mike Lindell and Kari Lake
Gun culture – the American Way
Will your kid come home today?
Most pressing issue of the day,
Drag shows! Hide your kids away!
Indicted ex-prez wreaking havoc
Yet people worry about a laptop
Guaranteed to take our country down –
Allegiance to a dangerous circus clown.

SOUND OFF

There are a lot of good things to read in Lovin' Life After 50. However, the pieces by Drew Alexander, "The Curmudgeon," are not among the worthwhile articles. This rabid right-wing ranter is a detriment to an otherwise basically good publication. He does not write about political issues but merely spews forth his own right-wing rants. It's quite offensive. His photo speaks volumes, just as The Donald's face bespeaks what lies within the man. If you must keep giving this "writer" space, at least counter with a column by an equally rabid liberal. Perhaps I will apply to balance things out.

REJECT ALL LIES

Re: the March 9 letter "Lies of Russia."

The letter talked about Putin's egregious lies being told to the Russian people about the Ukraine Invasion and war. It ended saying that Americans should be sure not to fall for these lies from Russia or any other country. A very large number of Americans bought, swallowed and still embrace the lies of Donald Trump including the Big Lie that the election was stolen. Serial liars Putin and Trump both count on and prey upon people who do not question the lies. The difference is that here in America, the truth is readily available for those who desire it and believe that the truth matters.

Published 3.14

THE HYPOCRISY OF SESSIONS, TRUMP

In his recent speech to the annual meeting of the National Association of Attorneys General, Attorney General Jeff Sessions pledged to "put the bad men behind bars." How soon will he lock up himself, Donald Trump, and the bigots, oil and coal magnates and climate and science deniers that make up the Cabinet?

The new head of the EPA has private email issues not unlike those of Hillary Clinton, having communicated and schemed with heads of fossil fuel companies to undermine government efforts to protect our environment. Where's the ruckus over those private emails? Surely Attorney General Sessions will take care of that.

A QUESTION FOR THE SENATORS

A question for Sen. Marsha Blackburn, Sen. Ted Cruz, and others of their ilk: What is a moron? If these shameful excuses for senators are struggling for an answer, they need only to look in a mirror.

AMERICA'S SHAME
EMBODIED BY THE GOP

I'm sick of seeing photos of Jacob Chansley, Arizona's own "QAnon Shaman" insurrectionist. Is he allowed to wear his silly costume in prison? Maybe his loved ones have packed it away for some future Halloween event.   Or they might donate it to a museum devoted to the demise of our democracy.

How ridiculous that Chansley is coddled and catered to, even transferred to another facility to accommodate his demands for organic food.   He should have been left to continue his hunger strike to its conclusion if he had the guts. Chansley and the other phony patriot insurrectionists were set in motion by their messiah Donald Trump (another phony patriot.)

Trump sat by, immensely enjoying watching his pack of rabid hyenas storm the Capitol and inflict serious violence and death. He was going to march with them. What happened?

Maybe his bone spurs were hurting. If this is not worthy of impeachment, what would be? Shame will forever stain those politicians who voted against impeachment, whether they feel shame or not.

CRIME AGAINST AMERICANS

A letter writer feels that the situation at our southern border ("since Joe Biden was elected") is the greatest crime ever perpetrated against the American people. As if there was no border issue prior to Biden! I disagree that this is the most egregious crime ever committed against the American people. That distinction belongs to those responsible for the Jan. 6 insurrection, when a sore loser president orchestrated and condoned a violent and deadly coup attempt to overthrow our government and destroy our democracy. Incredibly, the deranged, disgraced miscreant is vying again to be president with the support of his weak and cowardly party. Welcome to the Twilight Zone.

SANTA COMES EARLY FOR THE RICH

Merry Christmas , top 1 percent and super-rich, big corporations and CEOs! Santa, his hair strangely yellow, and his hoard of evil elves were very, very good to you, bringing your windfall of gifts in the wee hours of Dec. 20. I guess that's because you are so very good all year long – so diligent about raking in money, destroying the environment, and figuring out how to further enrich yourselves at the expense of anyone and everything.

If only the rest of us could get even a lump of coal instead of the destruction of sane government, clean air and water, good public schools, affordable health care, national monument land, consumer protections – the list is long. Keep a close eye on your Social Security and Medicare benefits. This greed knows no limits, and lies, smokescreens and fake facts are continually employed to hoodwink the not-so-cognizant (to put it in a nice way) among us. Merry Christmas to all, and to all a good night. Hope you can sleep.

CAPITAL TOURS SHOULD INCLUDE RIOT

The U.S. Capitol is reopening for public tours. Suggestion: during tours have several large screens showing nonstop video of the Jan. 6 attack on our Capitol. Let the visitors see up close, in technicolor and surround sound the violent mob on that day. Show the insurrectionists defecating in the halls, bludgeoning Capitol police, and destroying the premises while shouting their murderous intent and waving their Trump flags. Show the brave Capitol police trying to stop this attempted coup. Show the gallows set up for Mike Pence. On display should be a large plaque naming all politicians who tried to deny or whitewash the events of that day, including those who told us it was really just like any other tour day. Also on display should be a large photo of Sen. Josh Hawley giving the fist of support to the insurrectionists, and photos and names of everyone so far arrested. That day should never be forgotten, or perhaps worse, normalized.

NO BLAME, NO SHAME, JUST FLAMES

Re: the Aug. 14 letter "Climate change."

This letter gave new insight into Trump's claim some years back that he "loves the poorly educated". This letter denied any link between raging global wildfires and climate change and was a blanket disparaging of science and scientists. Shots were taken at Dr. Fauci, his fellow scientists, and the group Science Moms. Links between the fires and climate change were described as "baseless claims" and "only conjecture". Totally false and most people know better. The letter writer said science should not point fingers but just focus on solutions. Translation – ignore and bury the facts (which will expose culpability); deny the science behind the causes. Exposing facts is NOT finger pointing! Solutions can only arise from addressing the causes via science. We saw the results of science denial during the pandemic. Many refused the vaccine and masking, and for some, the result was death. I'm surprised this science-trashing letter didn't go further, by suggesting these climate catastrophes are some natural cycle, or maybe God's will.

August 17, 2023

On The Other Side
Of Life With
Horse Sense & A Tribute

FOR THE LOVE OF HORSES

I WAS BORN LOVING HORSES. Some people just have it ingrained and, I surely did. I can't explain where it comes from, as no one else in my family has the slightest interest in the animals. From my earliest years, I was drawing and coloring horses, getting excited at anything remotely horsey, and dreaming of a future that included these wondrous animals. As a child, I sometimes went to ride at the old Deem's Riding Academy, $2.00 per hour. Then in grade school and junior high it was Circle C and Ideal Academy. My best friend Suzie was just as horse crazed as I was, and we spent hours running thru the woods near our homes, whinnying, and playing with our plastic steeds. We cut out every magazine photo of a horse we found and made voluminous scrapbooks. Some weekends, if we washed and waxed my Dad's car, he'd drive us out to the riding stables and wait as we engaged in our hour of horse heaven. My Dad used to tell me, "You better marry a farmer."

Finally realizing that my parents were not going to buy me a horse, I bought my first at age 21. Of course at that age, I wasn't thinking about the cost of long-term horse boarding, nor could I foresee at the end of it all, I could have purchased our retirement home with what I spent on horses! But it was worth every cent to me. Zalton was wonderful, a tall lanky red chestnut half Saddlebred, half Arab. He was calm and trustworthy, and I rode him all over North Canton and Greentown. We even had one unusual adventure, when I found a woman who had overdosed and was unconscious in her car in an area I sometimes rode in. It was a very warm day, and all the car windows were up. When I opened her car door, she began to choke and gasp in the fresh air. Paramedics were hailed. I like to think maybe it was Zalton and me to the rescue, with a lot of help from the paramedics.

Late in his life, Zalton had a serious leg injury yet after a long time of healing still valiantly carried me around on my equine excursions, limping along with a withered leg.

I finally had to put him down after almost 20 years; it was devastating saying goodbye to my lifelong dream. He was soon replaced by the beautiful and elegant Lacey, a purebred Arab. She was a handful, but sweet, with a mind of her own and a little dose of brattiness. She also gave me so many hours of riding pleasure, as we explored trails and fields in all sorts of weather. I loved enjoying nature and the seasons from the backs of my trusty mounts — especially the fall with the leaves crunching underneath and the stops in old gnarly orchards where I'd let them enjoy some pocked apples. At age 23, arthritis became a problem for Lacey and the vet deemed her not safe to ride.

Shortly after I retired her to a quiet, serene private farm, she had a stroke while in the pasture. Her demise took way too long even with the vet's assistance, as she had almost no pulse to carry the life-ending drugs. Again, devastating.

My friend who boarded Lacey was kind enough to allow her burial on their property, which was comforting. She was laid to rest next to her friend "Chicka."

So, the end of a very long and fun and rewarding chapter of my life came to an end, just as my own health issues came to mean no more riding. And then, it was time to move to my new (horseless) life in Arizona. No door has opened to fill the void, yet. I miss those gorgeous horses – their velvet noses, snuffling for treats, their nickering in recognition when I walked into the barn, and the enjoyment of them carrying me all over creation. I hope they enjoyed it, too – I think most of the time, they did!

IN TRIBUTE TO THE MOST AMAZING LITTLE SQUIRREL... LEPPS

LEPPS CAME ONTO OUR DECK and into our lives in about 2003. And what a unique little squirrel she was! Diminutive in size, unique in color – a brownish charcoal colored coat with golden flecks. But most unique was her personality – demure, calm, trusting and peaceful. We named her Lepps because when her visitations began, she had a troublesome skin condition that we speculated was the equivalent of squirrel leprosy.

Over time, our frequent feeding of nuts and nutritious squirrel snacks cleared that up very well. The other squirrels weren't very nice to Lepps. They aggressively chased and bullied her, much to our dismay. However, Lepps soon learned to work with us, waiting demurely in a corner while we chased the others away, then resuming her peaceful snacking. She learned her name, and often waited on our lower patio for us to open the upper deck sliding doors and call "Come on, Lepps"! And up she'd pop, to entertain us again . We figured Lepps' brain was almost three times the size of the average squirrel's grey matter. Despite her lack of aggressiveness, she managed to thrive for at least seven years, visiting us regularly.

Each summer, she seemed to disappear for several months, which would send us into fits of sorrow, speculation as to her fate, and remorse that we might never see her again. And then, out of the blue, there she'd be, as we'd run and swoon and trip over each other to get her snacks.

She was a terrific mother and brought her many broods to our deck to show them the ropes. Many days, she'd come 3 to 4 times and often we'd delay our plans to stick around to cater to this remarkable little friend. Even if things were a bit rocky at home, Lepps could perk us up and return us to a more positive state. I'd often say, "that little squirrel has held a marriage together".

Fall of 2010 was an especially fantastic Lepps festival. Our little darling was coming each and every day, three times a day, and putting on performances that left us glowing inside. That was the last we saw her. Though our hearts are heavy, we know she lived a long and happy life, and that we were a part of that success. What we wouldn't give to see Lepps again, but alas, she lives only on my screensaver. Her offspring abound, however, some bearing quite a resemblance-- but none possessing that incredibly unique demeanor and personality, that intelligence and way of interacting, that belonged to their mother. May she rest in peace wherever she is!

I READ
BANNED
BOOKS
I READ
BANNED
BOOKS
I READ
BANNED
BOOKS

SESHAT (SASHET, SESHETA),
MEANING 'FEMALE SCRIBE',

SEEN AS THE GODDESS OF WRITING, historical records, accounting and mathematics, measurement and architecture to the ancient Egyptians. She was depicted as a woman wearing a panther-skin dress (the garb of the funerary stm priests) and a headdress that was also her hieroglyph which may represent either a stylized flower or seven-pointed star on a standard that is beneath a set of down-turned horns. (The horns may have originally been a crescent, linking Seshat to the moon… hence to her spouse, the moon god of writing and knowledge, Thoth.)

She was believed to appear to assist the pharaoh at various times, and who kept a record of his life.

It was she who recorded the time allotted to him by the gods for his stay on earth.

She was associated with the pharaoh at the 'stretching the cord' foundation ritual, where she assisted the pharaoh with the measuring process.

During New Kingdom times, she was shown to have been involved in the sed (jubilee) festival of the pharaohs, holding a palm rib to show the passage of time.

She kept track of each pharaoh and the period for which he ruled, and the speeches made during the crowning rituals.

She was also shown writing down the inventory of foreign captives and captured goods from campaigns.

- Cyril Fagan, Zodiacs Old and New (1951)